This Books Belongs To.........

....

....

....

Trace the steps for making the letter a on the following line.

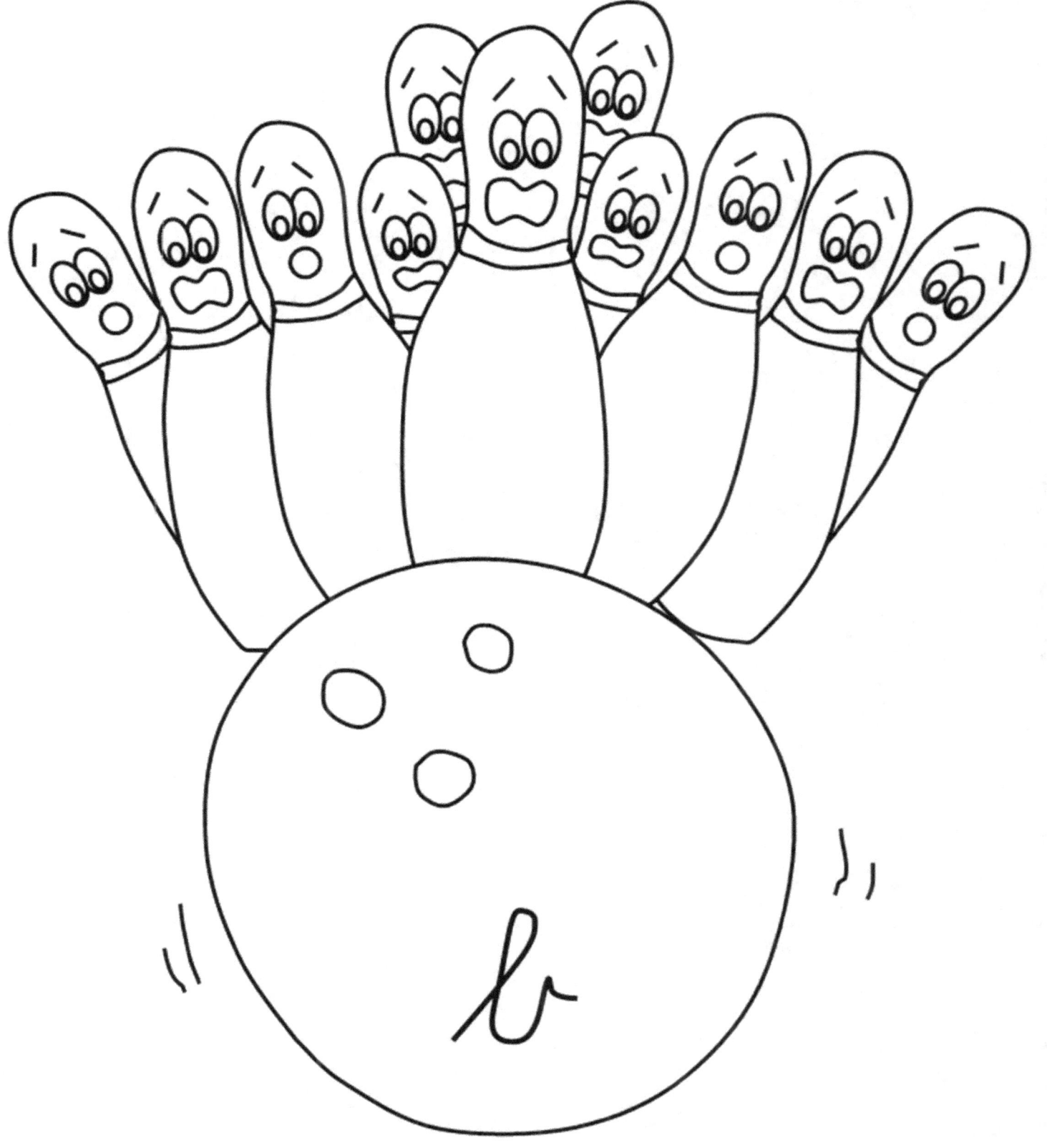

Trace the steps for making the letter b on the following line.

Trace the steps for making the letter c on the following line.

Trace the steps for making the letter c on the following line.

c   h   ch   ch   ch   ch

Trace the steps for making the letter d on the following line.

_ɔ_ _ɔ_ _d_ _d_ _d_ _d_ _dd_

Trace the steps for making the letter e on the following line.

Trace the steps for making the letter f on the following line.

Trace the steps for making the letter g on the following line.

Trace the steps for making the letter h on the following line.

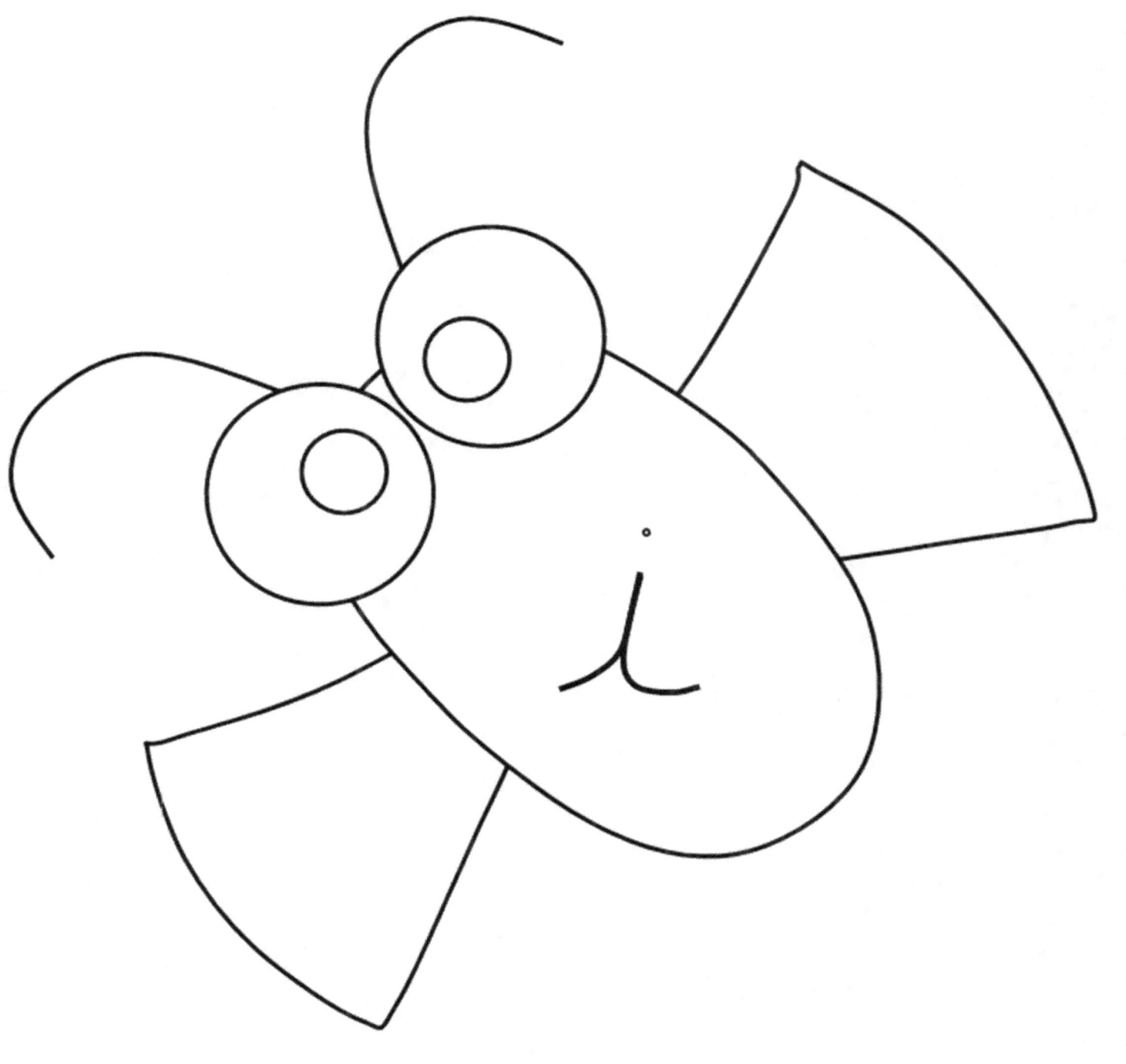

Trace the steps for making the letter i on the following line.

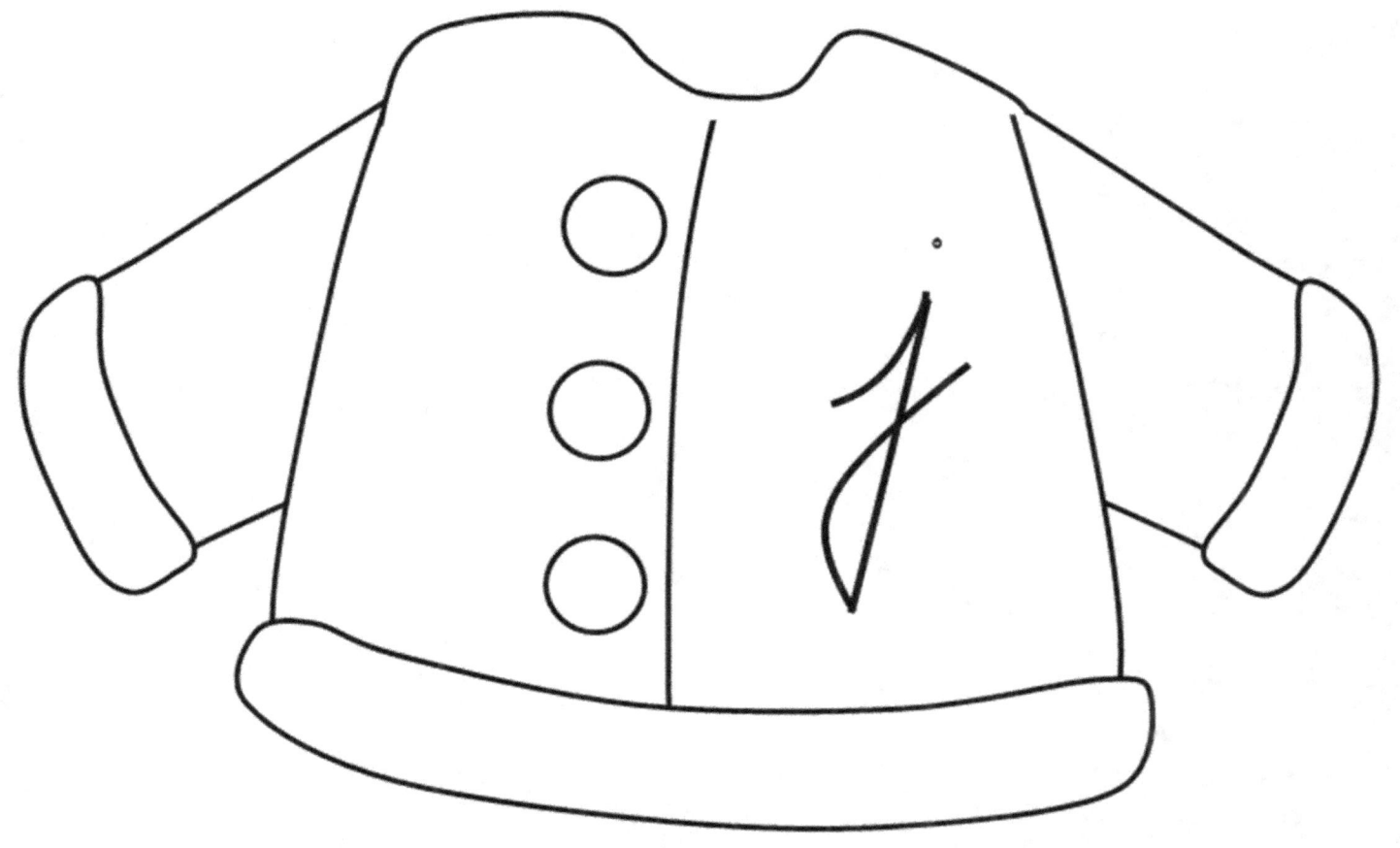

Trace the steps for making the letter j on the following line.

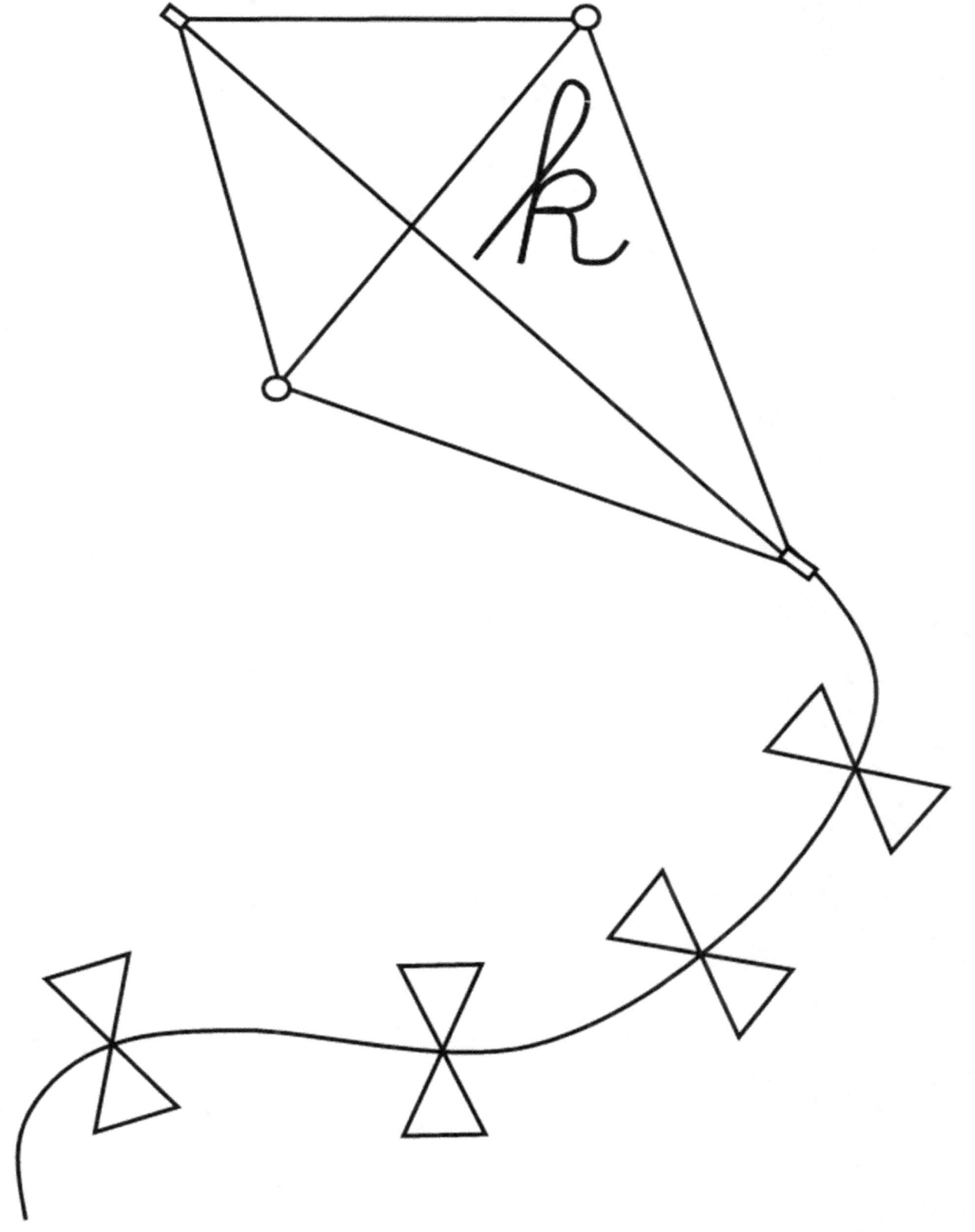

Trace the steps for making the letter k on the following line.

/   /k   /k   /k   /k   /k/k

Trace the steps for making the letter l on the following line.

Trace the steps for making the letter m on the following line.

Trace the steps for making the letter n on the following line.

Trace the steps for making the letter o on the following line.

Trace the steps for making the letter p on the following line.

p   p   p   p   p   p   pp

Trace the steps for making the letter q on the following line.

Trace the steps for making the letter r on the following line.

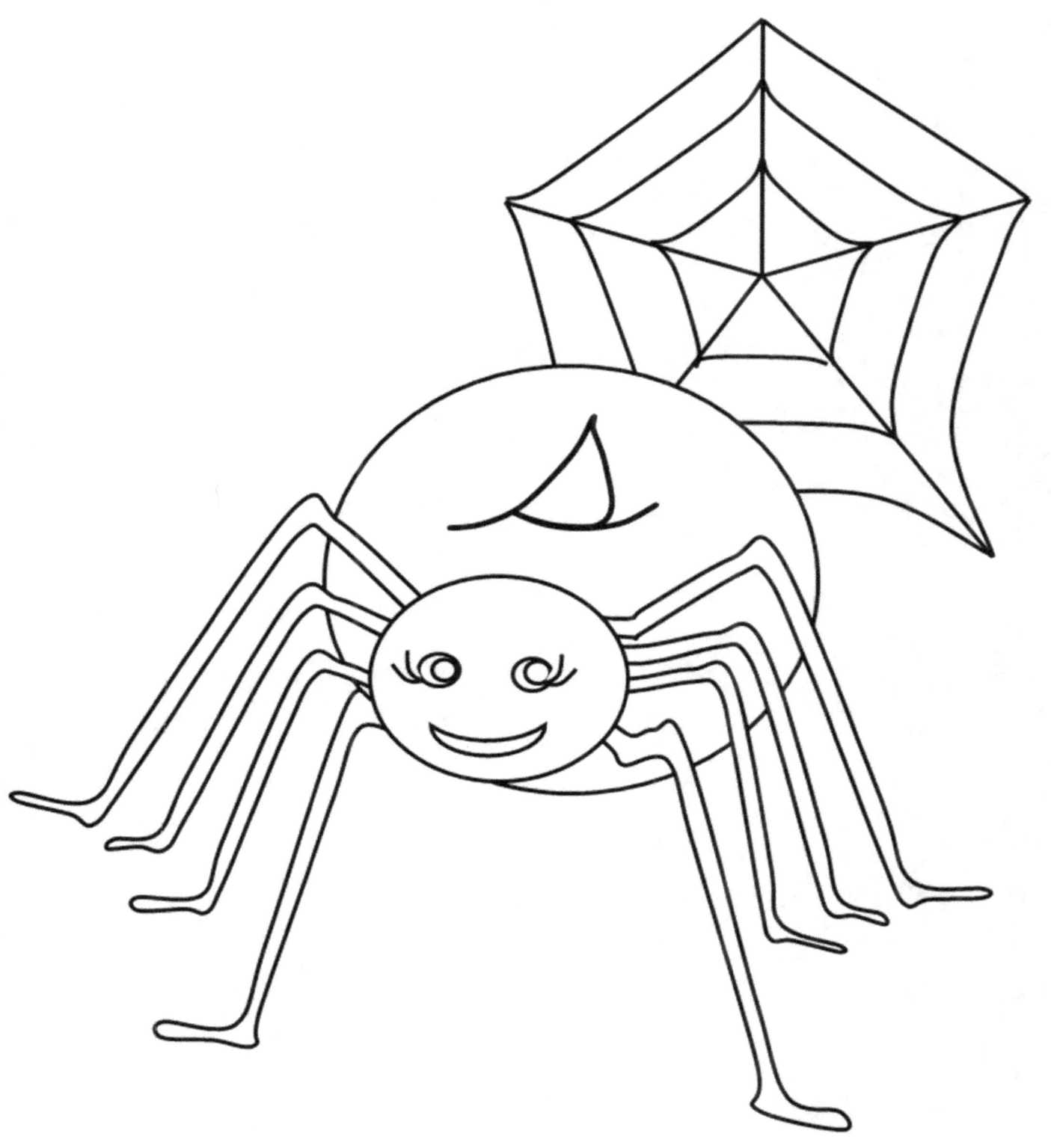

Trace the steps for making the letter s on the following line.

Trace the steps for making the letter sh on the following line.

_s_ _sh_ _sh_ _sh_ _sh_

Trace the steps for making the letter t on the following line.

Trace the steps for making the letter th on the following line.

t   h   th   th   th   th

Trace the steps for making the letter u on the following line.

Trace the steps for making the letter v on the following line.

Trace the steps for making the letter w on the following line.

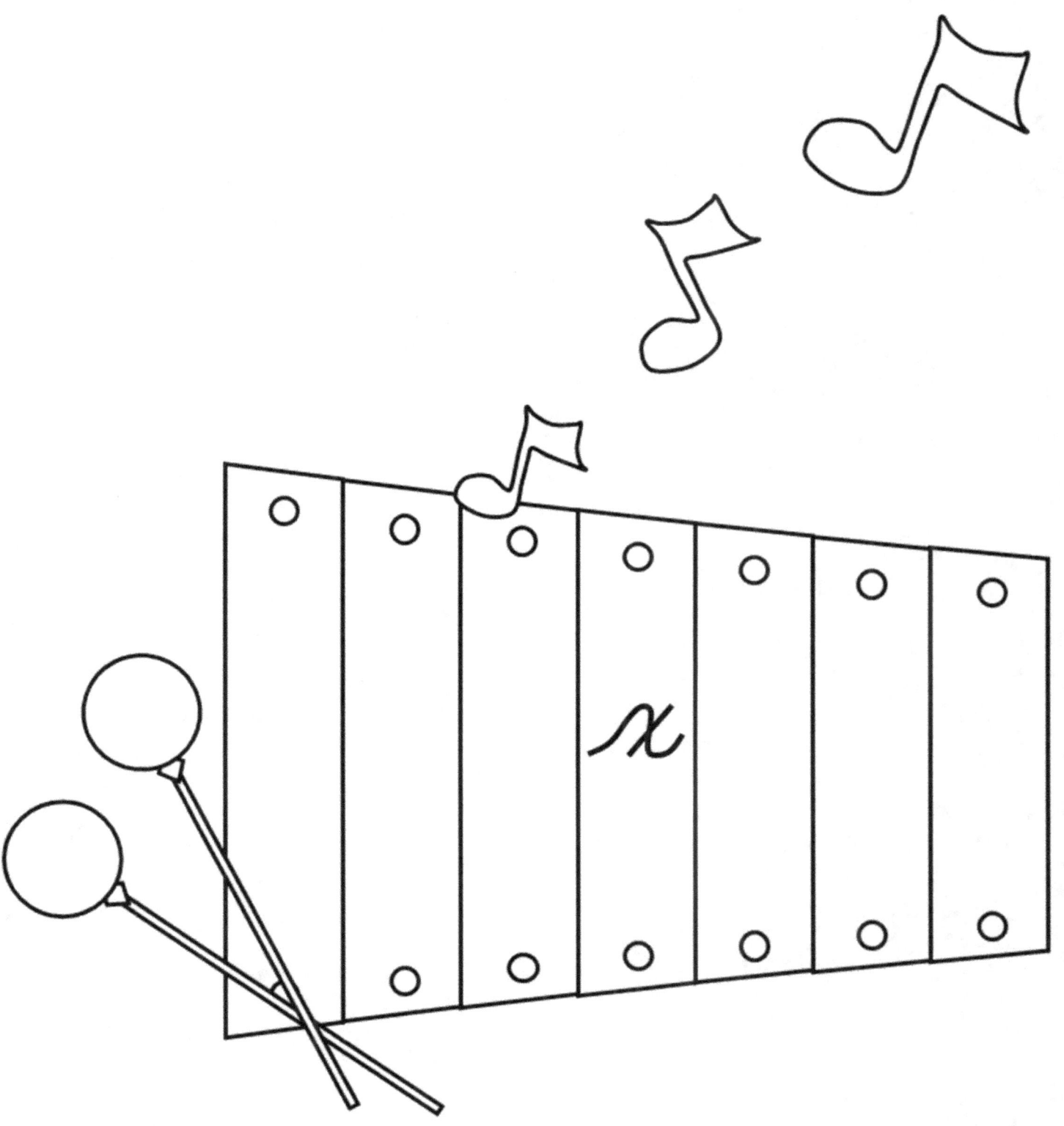

Trace the steps for making the letter x on the following line.

Trace the steps for making the letter y on the following line.

Trace the steps for making the letter z on the following line.